Mountains, Medicines and Miracles

by

Mollie Clark, MBE

Acknowledgements

This is a brief account of my own personal experiences in Bhutan and I want to express thanks to my many friends who over the years have encouraged me to write about these times.

My very grateful thanks to Joyce who painstakingly solved all my computer problems, sorted all the photos, and printed the whole thing more than once. She also came up with the very apt title.

My sincere and grateful thanks go to David Lewis who willingly added to his busy life by helping with tenses and grammar, and putting everything in order.

Thanks also to Christine Holmes who has helped with the final stages of the book production.

Front cover: Drugyel Dzong, Paro

ISBN 978-1-909075-74-0

Printed by:
Short Run Press Limited, 25 Bittern Road,
Sowton Industrial Estate, EXETER, Devon, EX2 7LW

Foreword

Bhutan is a fantastically beautiful country and home to a vibrant people. Mollie Clark is a remarkable woman with a strong faith and an indomitable spirit. Bring the two together and you have the makings of a truly fascinating story: a story of medical success, of human endurance and, most of all, God's amazing love.

This short but powerful story is a close-up account of the challenges endured by people who live in magnificent but remote valleys set in the Himalayan mountains. To be affected by leprosy in any situation presents huge barriers of misunderstanding, stigma and rejection. For the people of Bhutan, the added factor of isolation was yet another burden.

Mollie came into this situation as The Leprosy Mission was just beginning its work in partnership with His Majesty's Government in Bhutan in 1968 after working with TLM in India for eight years. It was a country that she came to love passionately and serve with honour.

The stories in these pages are of real people, so often suffering great hardships without the basic medical support most of us take for granted, but it is told with Mollie's irrepressible sense of humour which, on more than one occasion has, got her into some strife.

It was my great privilege to be present at Mollie's farewell from Bhutan in October 1986. The expressions of love and gratitude by the government for the work that The Leprosy Mission had done in the struggle against leprosy was so evident and obvious on that occasion.

The results in Bhutan remain one of the real success stories in leprosy, and stand as a wonderful example of excellent co-operation between a government and a Christian mission. Much of that success can be attributed to the hard slog in trekking over mountain passes, sleeping in flea-infested beds or on tea-shop tables by the young Bhutanese para-medics and the nurses, like Mollie, who trained and guided them.

Leprosy is now controlled in Bhutan, and one can only guess at the amount of human misery that has been avoided because of the work undertaken in the 1970s and 80s, but as you will read, this story is not just about leprosy. It is about meeting the needs of people wherever they are encountered, and that is the core of the Christian faith that motivated a young British nurse to undertake challenges that would deter the strongest man.

Ken Martin

Chairman,

The Leprosy Mission International

Preface

As I come towards a bend in the road, I look up from the rough unmade surface and see a man leading a well-laden pony. He is dressed in strange clothes and framed with a background of hills towered over by a snow-capped mountain. In the valley below is a crystal-clear river rippling over rocks and pebbles. I am amazed, for this is the picture I had in a dream a number of times as a child, and he is wearing the normal clothes for men in this country. If I have any doubts about whether this is the right place for me, they are immediately dispelled. What am I doing here in Bhutan anyway, at nearly 8,000 feet, since until a few weeks earlier I have been working on the hot plains of India?

During the months before I left school, I had no idea about the work I should do. Friends had already decided their careers, some going into offices, and some remaining at school to take their School Certificate, but this was not an option for me, as I had to go and earn my living. A few weeks before we were due to leave school, a lady came to the school and talked about the possibilities of nursing training. I immediately knew this was what I would like to do, but I was only 15, so too young to start training. With high hopes, I went to the employment exchange and was offered plenty of jobs in offices, shops, chemists, etc., but I refused, as I was determined not to work anywhere but in a hospital. After nearly three weeks they gave me a letter to the matron of one of the hospitals, and I happily went to give it to her. She saw me and offered me a job in a residential nursery that was part of the hospital, and this put me on the road to the rest of my life. As soon as I was old enough I did my general nurse training followed by midwifery training. During this time I became a Christian and after hearing a talk about leprosy, decided this was the work I should do. After some experience in midwifery I went on to do a course in tropical diseases, and then applied to The Leprosy Mission, and finally sailed off to India at the beginning of February 1961...

I spent eight years working with The Leprosy Mission, an international Christian organisation, in a large leprosy hospital in West Bengal. We treated and cared for patients and did what we could for them, but we really longed for the day when a cure would be found and leprosy eradicated.

There were about 700 inpatients and every day many patients came to the outpatient department.

At that time, the patients had very little hope of being cured and many stayed there most of their lives. The hospital was divided into different sections: one where the very disabled patients lived; another area was for children with leprosy, and also a school for them; and another for patients who were able to work in some capacity. The hospital was separate and was kept for patients who were very sick with other diseases, those with reactions to the drugs, and those recovering from surgery.

During the years I worked there, I was involved in many different aspects of the work, and it was a time of learning and gaining experience, as well as building up my faith for the next step in my journey through life. The very disabled patients were incredible! Some were blind, many had no fingers left, and just stumps for feet, but they looked after each other and showed such love and thankfulness for even the smallest things we did for them. I look back at that time with great affection for those lovely people.

Then, in 1968, soon after the mission had been invited by the Royal Government of Bhutan (a small Buddhist kingdom) to set up a leprosy control programme there, I was transferred and given a unique and wonderful opportunity to work in the country during the early stages of its development. This was part-way through the second Five Year Plan for socio-economic development in the country, concentrating on education, health, communication, agriculture and power. The first Plan was launched in 1961 with economic, financial and technical assistance from the government of India.

At this time, 1968-69, an Inner Line Security area was established along the whole of the North India border, and India advised Bhutan and Sikkim on foreign affairs as they were within the Inner Line. For this reason, we foreigners had to obtain a special Inner Line Permit in order to enter Bhutan.

Chapter One – Gida Kom

The journey to Bhutan is the start of my adventures. The flight, provided by a private airline, leaves Calcutta at 4.00 am. It is a small freight plane and today it carries seven passengers and lots of freight. Each passenger is weighed, together with their luggage. The freight is tied in the centre of the plane with the passengers seated around the edge.

En route for Bhutan, we land at two or three tea plantations where some of the freight is unloaded and a few passengers disembark. After the third stop, the door is stuck and will not close, but the pilot decides to take off anyway! At the next stop the pilot says he cannot fly into Bhutan because of bad weather. I find we have landed in a field where there is one small shed, and later find out it is about seven miles from the border of Bhutan. I am told I cannot get a taxi or a bus from here, and as I wonder what to do, along comes a jeep carrying a Scottish tea planter, who stops and asks me where I am going. When I tell him, he invites me to his home for breakfast and then says he will send me to the Bhutan border in his jeep. It is a wonderful offer that I gladly accept. He is like an angel in disguise to me!

A few years later, Bhutan has its own airline, Druk Air, with an 18-seater Dornier, which also gives us exciting trips in and out of Bhutan! It follows the river through a fairly narrow valley until it comes into the Paro Valley to land. Often it seems as if we will hit the side of the mountain as we are travelling, especially if it is a windy day.

Bhutan lies north of India in the eastern Himalayas and is a land of hills and valleys, quite awe-inspiring in its splendour, with majestic mountain peaks and lush fertile valleys, snow-covered mountains and forest-clad hills. The bus going up to Thimphu is packed and, as the road twists and turns ever upwards, the air becomes cooler. We wait at a number of places as there are landslides and these have to be cleared before we can go any further. I arrive at Gida Kom Hospital about nine hours later. Everything is completely different from India: the people, customs, culture, religion and languages, but I never feel a stranger.

Gida Kom is a small valley fifteen miles or so from Thimphu, the capital, and the hospital is situated about halfway down the valley at an altitude of about 7,500 feet.

Because there are few medical facilities in the country, we take on general medical work as well as the leprosy control programme.

For the next four and a half years or so I am based at Gida Kom Hospital, which opened only the previous year. The hospital has beds for leprosy patients and also some for general medical patients. Some of these are very sick – for example, one young girl has cirrhosis of the liver, and a man in his thirties has leukaemia. Another young girl with very advanced tuberculosis is not responding well to treatment. Some of the leprosy patients have terrible disabilities because of lack of treatment, and hopefully some will be able to have surgery to correct these later on. Some have ulcers due to anaesthesia of their hands and feet.

I have not been here long when I am called to a Tibetan village where a lady is having problems with the delivery of her sixth child. It is about an hour's walk from the hospital. I take a Bhutanese girl with me; although she understands very little English, she knows a little Bengali, which I had learned in India.

It is nearly dark when we reach the house, and inside it is black with soot from the fire. There is also a small container with burning chips of resin cut from pine trees that give a reasonable light and plenty of smoke. There are four children in the house, ages ranging from about three to fifteen. The father spends most of the night sitting by the fire with his prayer wheel chanting prayers. His hair is braided and deep lines etch his face, which appears quite stern until he smiles and then his whole appearance changes. After examining the woman I find there is no foetal heart and she says she has felt no movements for some time. After some hours the dead baby is delivered, and I feel sorry that my first delivery there is a stillborn, but the couple seem so grateful that I was there and are sure I have saved the mother's life! It is an amazing insight into a very different culture.

As we walk back to the hospital, when day is breaking, I think what an interesting situation I have just witnessed: not much more than a few words of language between us, and no doctor in the area should one be needed. This, I was to discover, would be a regular feature of life for me over the next few years.

After this I look for someone to teach me Dzongkha, and eventually find a fellow who says he will help me. It takes nearly an hour to reach him so I go whenever I can. I have to repeat everything he says, and every time I go, the audience seems to increase, and they find the lessons a very hilarious affair! I learn what I can, but realise again that language-learning is not one of my strong points!

At one time there is a bear roaming around at the hospital, and on another occasion we can see a tiger on the hill opposite the hospital, but that is the only time I see one, although we do sometimes see their footprints and droppings. There are plenty of different types of deer around. Sometimes people come and ask for help for their domestic animals. One old lady comes with her little dog whose back legs are paralysed. Another time someone brings their horse that has an injury and needs stitching! Then I am asked to go to a village to see a cow which they say has a retained placenta! When they see my hesitation, they also say the daughter has fallen off the roof and is injured, so I go. The daughter has a few cuts and bruises and is a bit dazed, but there are no broken bones. The roof is not very high. Then I reluctantly go to look at the cow, take hold of the cord, and hope and pray for the best. Fortunately, the placenta comes out with no problem and the family are happy, as they have a lovely healthy calf!

A lady who has been mauled by a bear comes to the hospital one day. Her eyelid and one of her cheeks is hanging off, but wonderfully the eye is not damaged. I set to and attempt to stitch her up; it takes ages to get it all clean and put together again. The smell is awful but, with a good dose of antibiotics, it heals well.

I am being called out more and more to deliver babies, and some are very difficult deliveries. I decide to start an antenatal clinic at the hospital, and also in one of the local villages, where some of the ladies have very bad obstetric histories, having lost a number of babies during birth. It is good to be able to keep my eye on them during their pregnancies. A couple of the mothers time their deliveries at the antenatal clinic, which saves me another trip!

Bhutanese mother and baby

One day I am called to the wife of the head man in one of the local Tibetan villages. She has been in labour for a few hours but eventually I deliver a good-sized baby boy and they are delighted. I cannot help contrasting the room with the sterile conditions in English labour wards. Strings of soot hang from the ceiling and the walls are black from the fire. Dogs, cats and chickens are roaming around, and one chicken hops nonchalantly onto the sterile instruments and out through the window just as the baby is being delivered. A few days later, I am asked to go to another village where a lady I have seen at an antenatal clinic has delivered her baby some days earlier but has a retained placenta. The baby is fine and I am able to deliver a very smelly placenta without too much trouble. I am always so thankful to God for safe deliveries, and for people recovering from their different illnesses.

Sometimes I go out with one or two paramedical workers to do a leprosy survey. We often go by jeep for part of the way, and we usually set up camp near a river. On one of these trips, we stop in a valley that is covered in primula, and is really beautiful. The river is crystal-clear, bouncing over rocks, with the sun glistening on it. We walk to the nearest village and complete the survey, finding new leprosy patients who we start on treatment, then return to camp as darkness falls. We cook a meal of rice, chillies and some vegetables, and afterwards go to our tents. As I say good night, I add that I hope it does not rain, as my tent leaks a bit. A big storm comes and I move from side to side to avoid the drips. Then I hear some noise and laughter from the other tent, and suddenly my wet tent collapses onto me. It seems my well-intentioned companions had decided to put a large, heavy tarpaulin over my flimsy tent. By the time they have helped me to extricate myself, we are all soaking wet and roaring with laughter! 'You will have to come in with us now,' they say, dragging out my wet bedding and placing it between them in their tent. After we have warmed up and all the giggling has stopped, we manage to get a good night's sleep. I have to buy a new tent after that!

Our aim is to find all the leprosy patients and put them on treatment, and we also examine as many of the relatives of the patients as we can. We then set off once again to a different area. We always need to take with us sleeping bags, medicines and food. These are packed in the jeep and off we go on a 2-3 hour drive. The road is rough in parts and rises to about 10,000 feet, winding round and round in hairpin bends. As we approach the top of the pass, a big notice warns us: 'Beware, road subject to icing'. There is a wonderful view from the top, looking over range after range of mountains, with snows in the background. We then descend to about 4,500 feet, and stop for a cup of tea in a small teashop, before carrying on a few miles to a small valley leading to the villages we are aiming for. We leave the jeep and walk up beside the river. It is so lovely, and we watch a couple of otters fishing in the river and see many birds on the way. The last part is quite a stiff climb up to the village. We find some patients and examine them and give them medicines. Then we make our way back, and since we are descending, the journey is much quicker. We have split into two teams; soon afterwards the other team arrives back and we continue on to the next area.

Tibetan mother and child

One cold February night I am called to see a young Nepali lady who is having labour pains although she is barely eight months pregnant. The family live in a wooden shack and it is bitterly cold. She delivers a tiny boy weighing two pounds who is having difficulty breathing, but as she is also having problems, I deal with her first and then the baby. I wrap him up in cotton wool and put a hot water bottle in his basket but think he will not survive. Over the next few weeks I am called to see him a number of times for various reasons but he starts to put on weight slowly, and eventually grows up to be a healthy boy and is now married with a family of his own. I always called him Tom Thumb!

A few months later, a Tibetan lady of about 20 is brought in with severe toxaemia of pregnancy. She is so swollen it is difficult to feel anything, but the people who have brought her in say she is about eight months pregnant. She delivers a tiny girl, with some help, but dies soon after. Evidently the husband deserted her three months previously and we are left with this wee thing. I wrap her up in cotton wool and put her in a basket by the fire. She is fed three-hourly day and night, but shows no interest in living. Then gradually she begins to gain weight (her birth weight was just over two pounds), and, contrary to everyone's expectations, she thrives. When she is just over three months old and about eight pounds in weight, her grandmother comes and takes her home. It is wonderful not to be woken in the middle of the night with her hungry howls but we all miss her gurgling smiles. She grows up into a lovely girl, and comes to see us at the hospital from time to time.

We are asked to do a survey in an area where two Swiss men are running a dairy farm, so one morning we set off in the jeep, and on the way drop off two paramedical workers in a different area. We meet our guide who has two horses and then set off on a track up the side of a hill. We reach where we are going to stay the night – a house perched on the side of the hill at about 5,500 feet, with a lovely view along the valley. We see a few folk who are sick and give them treatment, while we are given the usual butter tea and flattened rice. Rinchen, our guide, takes us out to show us the mountain we have to climb the next day, and says, 'It is very difficult.' Then, after an enormous meal of rice, vegetables and eggs, I am given the best room in the house. I lay my sleeping bag on the floor and stretch out under the gaze of Lord Buddha who is sitting in position on the large family altar which fills one side of the room.

Next morning we leave early after another big meal of rice and start going up through the forest. There are orchids growing in such profusion and breathtakingly lovely. The path is very narrow and wet and muddy, with a long drop on one side. We go up and up and the air becomes colder. The rhododendrons are in bloom and violets cover the banks. The only sounds to be heard are occasional birdsong, our heavy breathing, and the clip-clop of the horses. We go on and on until we come out of the forest onto a lush plateau at over 9,000 feet. It is really beautiful with primula, violets, gentians, rhododendrons and wild roses growing in abundance. We follow a clear crystal stream that is rushing over rocks and boulders, and after a while sit down to rest and eat beside it. Then we start again, up and up through a very cold, dark forest, fording streams with lichen-covered banks and stumbling over boulders, until we finally reach 11,000 feet. Then we begin to descend slowly, and as we do, we have a glimpse of a large valley ahead – lush, green and beautiful.

After we have finished a meal and then treated quite a number of sick folk, I am asked if I would like a hot bath and I jump at the opportunity, as it does not happen very often! I am shown where to go and I find a huge wooden tub outside a building beside a stream of water. Four men are there carrying buckets filled to the brim with steaming water. One of them asks if it is the right temperature. I feel it and say it is wonderful, but would they mind first putting the bath inside the building? They look absolutely dumbfounded, and finally one says in his best English, 'But all mens take bath here'! I reply that I am not in the category of 'all mens', and anyway, I really do not fancy bathing on the open hillside, especially as it is raining! The altitude is 9,600 feet, the air is very cold, and I really want to make the most of this bath! They eventually decide that perhaps it is not quite the thing, as I am a queer kind of species, and they carry the bath into the building and fill it to the brim before going off. There is a huge wood fire blazing, and it is absolute bliss to indulge in this wonderful hot bath. We spend the next 2-3 days treating patients, and also find some new leprosy patients in the area, and put them onto treatment. It is a lovely valley and quite flat, so much easier for walking to see the patients, and the return journey back to the hospital is quicker as we are going downhill most of the way.

We know there is a higher incidence of leprosy in East Bhutan, and the Government ask if we will start work there at some time. Some of the paramedical workers had previously gone over to do surveys. I had also gone a couple of times, and we had always found more patients. A few patients had walked over to Gida Kom from the east, and told us they had walked for about 3-4 weeks, so we know there is a need there. A site is given for the building of a new hospital in a place called Mongar. Until arrangements are made for building work to begin, the Government have also given us the use of the old dispensary buildings for our immediate use.

In preparation for the move, we send a number of young men to train as leprosy paramedical workers to a Leprosy Mission hospital in India, so there will be a small group of workers to start some of the village work. As the work at this hospital at Gida Kom is now well established, and there are sufficient staff here, I am free to move to the east and help to set up the work there.

Chapter Two – Mongar

My move to Mongar coincides with the arrival of another nurse from England, Joyce Missing. It is anticipated that we will be living and working together for the foreseeable future. I find out very quickly that Joyce is good at the things that I struggle with, so we complement each other in the work. She settles in very quickly, even though this is her first overseas posting, and she is soon well immersed in the work. It is also very good to have someone to discuss various problems with. The Government have given us the dispensary, a small ward, and two living quarters. They have very kindly built a bathroom onto the house where we are staying. The hospital site is about 300 feet lower than the dispensary, at about 5,500 feet in altitude. It is just near the township, which at that time consists of a dzong which is the administrative centre of the district and has a monastery at its centre, a police post, a wireless station, a school, a post office, an agricultural farm, three or four shops and a helipad. It will no doubt expand a lot over the next few years. Mongar itself is a large district, and we also look after the district north of here, where there is a higher percentage of leprosy.

The lateral road from the west to the east of Bhutan is being built, and in order to get to the east we have to travel from Thimphu south to Phuntsholing, the border town, and then travel by road through West Bengal and Assam to the east to Samdrup Jongkhar where we sometimes spend the night. (*See map at the back.*) Next day, we travel north up towards Tashigang, on the way calling in to see some Norwegian friends who run a school for the blind, and a hospital. Sometimes we will spend the night with them, depending on the state of the roads, and what time we arrive. The third day, we continue on the road until we reach Mongar.

Our house is just below the school and soon after it gets light in the morning we hear the songs of the children, as they study for their lessons that day. They read in a sing-song way, often a group of them together, which we soon get used to. Patients also start arriving from about 7 am for treatment. They leave their bundles piled up by our door, peer through the windows, and some come in and have a look round. They are very friendly, and perhaps the novelty of having us around will wear off before long. While it lasts, patients come in large numbers to the dispensary.

The ward has no beds but we have taken medical supplies with us; there are also a few medicines and plenty of lotions and potions left there, supplied by the Health Department. As soon as we arrive, patients start coming, and since we are near the school, lots of children come with different ailments and injuries. Many of them have intestinal worms and quite a number are anaemic. The ward is quickly filled with patients with many diseases: leprosy, tuberculosis, heart disease, burns, kidney infections, while sometimes a pregnant lady may come. We start to survey all the children in the schools throughout the district for leprosy and other diseases, and also give some health education. There is a completely different language here, and nothing in writing, but the good thing is the children in school are taught in English, and have Dzongkha lessons, so – as long as a schoolchild is around – we can make ourselves understood. Most of the staff also speak a number of languages, English being one of them, but we are attempting to learn as much as we can of Shachopkha, the local language.

The post comes by mail jeep 2-3 times a week, although when there are landslides, which are frequent, especially in the rainy season, a postal runner brings the mail, sometimes taking a few days. Often, when we have been doing village work, a postal runner will join us on the way to deliver mail to some of the villages. It is a hard job for them, and I sometimes wonder what kind of adventures our letters have on their journey here! Bhutan joined the Universal Postal Union in 1969, but a formal postal system had been introduced about 1962. They have always produced amazing stamps, much sought-after by many philatelists.

Physically the work can be quite hard, but it is very rewarding, and I would not change it for anything. As I was going into a village once, two elderly ladies exclaimed, 'How beautiful your hair is. Just like our grandmother Decchen's used to be!' On enquiring about this grandmother, I am told she had died many years ago, as she was a very old lady! I decide it is a rather back-handed compliment, if ever there was one. It is the first and only time in my life when anyone has complimented me on my hair! The local people are really great folk and very friendly.

There is no glass in our windows but wooden slats that have to be pulled back to let in the light, except in my bedroom, where the window is like a big wooden trellis with no glass or shutters. Someone has given us a little black hen and she starts hopping through one of the holes into my room and laying her eggs in one of my shoes each morning!

A patient keeps coming with a blocked nose, and nothing seems to help him. Amongst all the stuff in the dispensary is a jar of menthol crystals, so we decide to give him an inhalation with some of these in hot water. We sit him down and cover his head with a towel and he starts breathing in the vapour. Suddenly we hear an almighty sneeze, followed by many more! It seems to go on and on. I have a fit of the giggles, which is a regular thing with me, and a few others there follow suit! Eventually the fellow stops sneezing and says the medicine has cured him and he goes off a very happy man! I do not remember him coming back with the same complaint again.

The building work and water supply gradually take shape, and we recruit and train more staff for the hospital work and the leprosy control work. When the hospital is complete, we are able to move the patients into the more spacious hospital buildings and vacate the dispensary. A doctor has been appointed, along with other staff, so the hospital is soon full and busy with many outpatients coming each day.

One day a man comes to the hospital bringing his son, a lad in his early twenties, who has been gored in the abdomen by an ox. Evidently, the father says, his guts came pouring out, so the father took a hair from the horse's tail and an old needle, pushed the guts back in and put a few stitches in to hold the flesh together, put him on the horse's back and brought him on the long trek to the hospital. It just so happens that an Indian surgeon is visiting from Tashigang, so in the operating theatre he takes out the stitches, pulls out the guts and examines them. He finds that there are a few bruises but no perforation, so he cleans everything up and stitches him up again! The wound heals well, and after about two weeks, he walks back to his home. They need to be tough, living here!

We are called to a village not too far away where we are told seven children have died recently and a number more are sick. It turns out to be measles, while whooping cough is also a big problem, so we manage to obtain a supply of vaccines, and after this begin to do a regular vaccination programme in the villages around.

Quite a number of people come with injuries resulting either from chopping wood, or from a fall. One young fellow is saved from injury when one of the paramedical workers sees him trying to saw off a branch from a tree when he is actually sitting on the branch he was cutting, so tells him in no uncertain terms what will happen when the branch comes off! Some are injuries from animals, including a man injured by a wild boar. He spends many weeks in hospital.

The Sunday School in my church in England decided they wanted to put their collections each week towards buying a horse or two, because of all the village work we were doing. When we received their gift, we realised we could buy two horses with the money, and this we did. The children asked us to call them Bill and Ben! We eventually needed to buy more as it was easier to have our own on site than rely on local people to act as porters, as they were not always able to come when we needed them. When any of us went to the villages, we had to take quite a number of loads with us – bedding, food, medicines and so forth – so everyone was grateful for the ponies.

The Government is planning to set up basic health units all over the country, and to this end they start a Health School in Thimphu to train health assistants, auxiliary nurse midwives and basic health workers. We send seven of the local Bhutanese for various training and look forward to their return as there is a lot of work, both in the hospital and in the villages. A WHO advisor has been travelling around the country to check on the existing dispensaries with a view to possibly upgrading them to Basic Health Units. She comes to our area and also wants to go to Lhuntse. I am asked to travel with her. It is a good trip, and I really enjoy the scenery on the way. There has been an early snowfall and the hills look wonderful with their covering of snow. The mornings are crisp and clear with heavy frosts, and the days are perfect for walking. We camp each night, putting our tents up near a river or stream. When we are in Lhuntse, we are offered a room to sleep in, which I think will be more comfortable. I am woken up by a terrible noise, and it takes me a moment to realise it is snoring coming from the other bed! I have never heard such a racket from such a small lady as this. It goes on for most of the night and it is hard to get off to sleep again. After that, we go back to tents, and on our return journey, I make sure we stay near a noisy river if possible! It is just before Christmas when we get back and I keep in front of everyone and set a faster pace so that we arrive on Christmas Eve just before some of the staff have organised a carol service. We have 2-3 days to rest and replenish supplies before heading off in the opposite direction. This is to the south which is much warmer, as it is mostly walking along by the river, but this too is a worthwhile trip. We enjoy seeing a family of otters playing on the rocks beside the river.

One young woman comes to the hospital with a very badly burnt arm, bringing her two small children with her. Her husband is already in hospital having treatment for tuberculosis. One day he becomes violent, and after beating her, disappears and is not seen again. Her burns are quite extensive but slowly begin to improve. One leprosy patient who is admitted is very thin, disabled and has many ulcers. These slowly heal and he is then able to have surgery for a tendon transplant on both legs, and an operation on one eye so that he is able to close it again. With rest and a regular diet, he goes home looking well and nearly twice the size he was when he first came to the hospital! We thank God for all these successes.

In her spare time, Joyce has started giving English lessons to some of the staff children here: two small Finnish girls, three small Mizo boys, and some Nepali children. It is supposed to be for about half an hour most days but some of them spend a lot longer in the house.

Someone gives me a little Tibetan dog, a puppy. She is called Topsy, and over her lifetime produces a number of puppies. She is quite good company and always wants to accompany me when I am doing any village work, which is not very satisfactory. However, sometimes she manages to escape from the house – unbeknown to anyone – and follows me. On long trips I usually ride one of the horses when we are going uphill, and Topsy will run on ahead, climb on a rock, and cleverly manage to jump onto the saddle as I am passing! She has usually got herself very wet and muddy before that, so I am also very wet and muddy! The amazing thing is she never misses the saddle! She is a very determined dog, and when anyone begins to pack, whether it is Joyce or me, or any visitor, she will sit on the sleeping bag and refuse to move. When shifted, she somehow manages to look the picture of misery: she never wants to be left behind!

For some time we have been planning to start more intensive work in a place called Lhuntse, four days' walk north of Mongar. Two paramedical workers have been doing some leprosy work there but there is a need for more general medical care and community health. There is a Government dispensary there which is being upgraded to a Basic Health Unit, and we are asked to put staff there. I go up to look into a water supply, and the possibility of putting up one or two buildings. The mule track is hardly ever flat; we go up, and then, before long, start the walk down! It is a nice trip with the main river often in view. We cross over many smaller rivers and streams, where the water is crystal-clear, and often waterfalls cascade down into shimmering pools. We sometimes pass through pine forests and at other times through long lemongrass. It is a wonderful walk in the clear mountain air, with the scent of pines and the lemongrass, surrounded by incredible beauty and an amazing silence. Some of the bridges are good, but it takes all the courage I have to put a foot on others. I understand why the locals hang prayer flags from them!

In this same area is an old leprosy colony that was started by the Government. The incidence of leprosy is higher here than in other parts of Bhutan. I make several trips over the years to see what needs to be done. We visit all the patients who were originally in the colony. The old dispensary building is in a bad state of repair, and the patients have built little bamboo houses for themselves over the hillside. Their situation is dire: they are nearly all badly disabled but manage to grow a small amount of crops – including the chillies that are eaten in abundance by nearly everyone in Bhutan. We find new patients to put on treatment and are able to assess the situation before returning.

When we walk near the river on our way to this area, we pass some high cliffs on the opposite side of the river. Near the top of these are a number of very large beehives that appear to be hanging very precariously from the rocks. I have seen one or two in different places, but these seem to be larger. One of the Bhutanese tells me that in order to extract the honey they tie a long piece of string to an arrow and shoot it into the bees and catch the honey in a container! I never witness anyone doing it, but we are sometimes given fresh honey.

Once the hospital in Mongar is running well and fully staffed, Joyce and I are free to move to Lhuntse and start the work there. At 5-6,000 feet this is about the same altitude as Mongar, although the mule track goes up and down all the way as we make this journey. In fact, it is difficult to give definite altitudes as there are some very high hills throughout the districts, but because Lhuntse is north of Mongar, we used to have frosts where we were, and the high hills around had snow in the winter.

Lhuntse

Chapter Three – Lhuntse

Finally, after about five years of travelling backwards and forwards from Mongar to Lhuntse, Joyce and I do the four-day trek, and move here. We bring everything we need for living, from medicines, bedding, pots and pans to food. I have moved many times in my life but never in this way. We have five horses, six porters, two dogs, and some chickens! The path is not in a very good condition due to the long and heavy rainy season we have had, so it is quite hard going in parts. In one place it is very muddy and the smallest pony slips and falls a few feet into a rice field – with his loads. We quickly get the loads off and he soon jumps up, apparently none the worse for his fall. The loads, apart from being covered in mud, are also intact. At one place, the path is directly over the river, and above it are overhanging rocks. It is not wide enough for the pack horses to pass unless their loads are taken off. Some of the paths are quite treacherous in places with loose rocks and stones so it is easy to slip and stumble. For a long way we follow the main river where we often see otters. At night we camp and wash in the river, which is icy cold. One kind hen lays an egg most days on the way which we share and eat with our rice and vegetables. We arrive safely four days after leaving Mongar.

Ready to move

We have a house but no furniture apart from two bamboo chairs that we brought with us, and for a time things are pretty basic, but slowly everything comes together. On one of my previous trips, a fellow put together three planks to make a bed for me, one more than an inch lower than the others and one curved, and he hammered on some legs that stuck out in all directions. However, it is a bed, while Joyce has to be content with two doors, one on top of another, but they are neither long enough nor wide enough for her. Eventually a carpenter makes us beds and a table, and it soon seems like home. On the way up, we meet the postmaster for the district, a very nice man, and he promises to put a post-box on the wall of the dispensary building where we can post our letters. He also arranges for the postal runner to deliver our mail and collect what is in the box to save us walking to the post office, which he very kindly does. We are saddened to hear some time later that he has died in an accident.

The only water supply is a little stream running down the side of the hill through rice fields, but it is sometimes very muddy and has to be carried to the houses and dispensary, so a clean piped supply needs to be arranged as soon as possible. The local people seem very happy that we have come to stay, expressing their kindness to us by bringing us eggs and vegetables.

We start to get the old dispensary cleaned up and, as best we can, fumigated from the multitude of fleas, and reorganise it until we can get repairs and renovations done. There is a constant stream of patients, some of whom need to be admitted, but we have no beds or facilities to cater for them. However, the Bhutanese are very resilient and they all have at least one family member with them to look after them until we have the place properly up and running. One small boy of about 9 or 10 has been ill at home for three years. His lower spine, hips, knees and ankles have been affected by tuberculosis and he is in a very distressing condition, with a large ulcer and deep wounds on his back. He is such a brave little fellow, but we think only a miracle can help him.

Our work here consists of leprosy control in the whole district, which is up to three to four days' walk in all directions; treating outpatients as they come and looking after any inpatients; ante-natal care and child care in the immediate vicinity; and general community health. There is a lot to do, but we have with us three paramedical workers and four general helpers, one of whom was a patient in Gida Kom, but wanted to move with us first to Mongar and then here to Lhuntse, as his home is in this district. He is invaluable as he speaks so many languages; here in this district there are two main languages, and one large village has a different one! This

34

is my fourth language area, and language-learning is not one of my strong points.

One day I meet one of the Jesuit priests who work in this country. He runs an agricultural farm and is from Holland. He tells me he becomes a little tense sometimes and his blood pressure goes up, so he has been advised by one of the brothers to take 'a little compost'. '*What?*' I exclaim, horrified. 'A little compost, not much, maybe once a week or even less,' he says. Well, I think I know people do some strange things, but even if he is an agriculturalist, that is really over the top! So, trying to be tactful, I suggest he has a check-up and gets some decent tablets. 'Oh these tablets are good, let me show you,' he says. Then he puts his hand in his pocket and brings out a packet of *Calmpose*, a tranquiliser! I begin to wonder if the language problem is my hearing or my brains!

The Government asks us if we will do a systematic total population survey of the whole district, which fits in well with the leprosy surveys. Bhutan has a scattered rural population and this district is no exception, so Joyce and I decide we will take it in turns to go out for about two weeks at a time with a small team, while the other one stays at the hospital, dealing with all the patients who come. It is tough going, but very worthwhile, and we meet some incredible people. At night, we stay in a house in the village with one of the locals and try to examine all the people in the village, family by family. When it is dark, we have a meal of rice and chillies and then put our sleeping bags around the fire with all the family. It is very cold in the higher regions but pleasant when we are lower down. Eventually the survey is complete, all new leprosy patients are put on treatment and we treat many other sick people. We complete all the details of the survey and send them to the Department of Health.

Each year, Bhutan has three days of celebration for National Day. His Majesty the King of Bhutan goes to a different district every year to celebrate with the people and hold talks. Everyone around becomes very excited when they hear he is coming to the district where we are working, and great plans are made for the event. They are preparing an area about four hours' walk from our base for the event, and the *Dzongda* (head man) of the district asks us to go and stay at the dispensary to deal with any sick folk during those days, as most of the population of the district are expected to be there, he thinks. We are happy to oblige. He then asks us if we will make some cakes. We try to hide our looks of horror and reply feebly, 'We could try!' We have a temperamental kerosene stove, a tin box for an oven, and a cookery book. Neither of us is a cook! We have sugar, fat, non-vegetarian flour, i.e. full of weevils and other creatures, so we set to work. After a while there is a smell of burning, and we pull out a shrivelled burnt offering! We try twice more, and each time produce, instead of a lovely sponge, two looking like pancakes! We cut them up and called them 'King's rejects'! We think we should try once more and this time produce something that looks more like a cake, although a bit pathetic. We hand it over, and are very glad not to see it on the King's table!

When we arrive, we are amazed to see so many people. They have set up little camps all around the area, lit fires and are cooking their food. We go to the dispensary and leave our bedding and extra medicines there, before strolling round to see what is going on. We meet a few people we know and chat with them before it gets dark and we return to the dispensary. In the morning, just as I am waking up, there is a knock on the door, and I think that the patients have started to come, but rather it is a message with an invitation to an archery match and lunch with the King. It is a lovely time when we talk and have coffee in a very informal way, and later enjoy a wonderful buffet meal. The next day His Majesty addresses the crowds gathered from the whole district. Lunch is served to everyone, and those who are very poor are given a new article of clothing. We are very impressed by all of this and once again have the pleasure of dining with the royal visitors, who express their appreciation of the work of The Leprosy Mission. Then, after all the excitement, it is back to work.

One of the great benefits of the visit of the King is that a road will be constructed from Mongar to Lhuntse. Although we do not know how long it will take, we are all very pleased. We spend so much time walking, but although it is enjoyable, we realise there would be more time available for patients with a motor road to get us around. The dispensary is being upgraded to a small hospital, and a water tank is being built but because of the distance for ponies and porters to carry the building materials, everything takes time.

We try to do some regular health education in the local school, and with help from some of the schoolboys we also do it in the form of drama, which is very popular with the local people too, and hopefully they all learn something.

The Government has started National Service for graduates returning to Bhutan after studying in India or overseas. They have to do a six-month stint in some kind of community work before starting work in their chosen profession, and from time to time we are given two to work with us. On the whole, they do very well; digging latrines, doing health education and helping out where it is needed, and we appreciate them and all their efforts.

One day when I am returning to Lhuntse from Mongar, two of the students come with me. We are told if we go as far as we can on the new motor road that is being built, it will take us three hours less walking, which sounds good to us. So the horses and porters go on ahead with the loads, and we arrange to meet them by about 5 pm at a place by the river. We start off and follow the motor road, which is very dusty, and quite boring I think, until we come to a place where we have to leave the road. One of the road workers shows us a little path and tells us if we follow it upwards we will reach the mule track. So we take to the path which goes up and up, and finally seems to come to an end! We decide to carry on upwards for a while until we reach a sheer rock face, and can go no further, so go around it and start to descend a bit as we eventually need to reach the river. It starts to rain and we slip and stumble along, one of the lads twists his knee and the other one has cramp in his leg. Every now and then we have to wade through a stream and, as it starts to get dark, we find it more difficult, although we have a couple of torches with us. We find a small path and struggle along on that, finally reaching the river and our companions at 8 pm, hungry and exhausted. We collapse by the fire, have tea, rice and chillies, and are soon fast asleep. My sleeping bag has never felt so comfortable!

It is hard to make a move next morning, and we feel very stiff, but as we set off, the sun comes up and our wet clothes dry off as we walk. It is good to be on the mule track that I know so well, and the morning is very pleasant. We stop for lunch and soon afterwards we are crossing over a bridge that consists of three planks of wood, when one of the horses puts his foot through a hole and is balancing very precariously on the bridge. We try to get the loads off, but we cannot get the horse out of the hole. We manage to borrow a crowbar and ropes, and finally lever him out and get him on his feet, apparently none the worse for his ordeal! We eventually finish the trip without any other incidents and breathe a sigh of relief to arrive safely back.

On another trip, I am travelling with two different graduates. Before I leave Mongar, someone gives me a bar of chocolate that I put in the bag I carry, together with a book, a small umbrella, a torch and a water bottle. It is an extremely hot day, and we walk for a long period in the valley near the river. We pause by a little stream to try and cool off, and I take out my water bottle and it is covered in chocolate! The bar of chocolate has melted and everything in the bag is smothered in it! The lads say, 'We will help you clean it up,' and one takes the book and one the torch and we all start to lick! The one with the book turns to me with a look of great pleasure on his face, and says, 'Sister, this is the sweetest book I have ever read!' Everything is put back in the bag, and after washing in the stream, we carry on our journey.

We have to bring a lot of food like rice, flour, oil etc., and also kerosene up from Mongar as it is difficult to buy much here, and we are feeding patients too. Unfortunately, the kerosene is sometimes put on the same horse as a sack of food which means we have kerosene-flavoured flour or whatever the sack is carrying – not very pleasant! We use the kerosene for the lamps so it is important to always keep a supply here. The food is the usual rice, vegetables and chillies, and sometimes I long for something different.

Every now and again I would say to Joyce how lovely it would be to have some fruit or whatever it was I fancied that day. Often someone turns up for treatment with whatever it is, and we really enjoy it. One morning I really have a longing for an apple. There are lovely apple orchards in Thimphu but I have not seen any in this area. Fruit tree planting did begin in Bhutan after the country joined the Co-operative Economic Development in South East Asia in about 1963, and some trees were planted at Gida Kom after that. Anyway, later on that day, an Indian Army man who was working on the northern border calls in on his way to Mongar. He has four apples in his hand that a lady on his way down has asked him to bring down and give to me. I had seen her on one of my visits to her area. We are really thrilled and enjoy the apples very much. We feel that God is really looking after us! Another time, someone comes with some Swiss chocolate which is such a treat!

As well as the patients who need to be admitted for treatment, we also have many outpatients who come with all manner of things wrong with them. One young lad has a huge splinter about five inches long in his buttock which it is quite difficult to extricate, although we manage eventually. Quite a lot come with injuries, some needing suturing, many with dysentery and intestinal worms, coughs, urinary infections and skin infections. There are also those with heart disease and kidney disease. Each day is different and brings its own challenges. Some also need a tooth extracted, which I am not good at, but either Joyce or one of the paramedical workers always manages it! We have a number of difficult maternity cases who come to us, or we are called to their village. Life is never boring.

When Joyce is away for a few days, I am asked to go to see a lady who I am told has been in labour five days with her third child. When I arrive, I see that it is one of the leprosy patients who is very disabled, and she looks dreadful. There is no foetal heart or movement and she dies without delivering her baby. I feel angry and distressed. If we had known she was pregnant, we could have arranged for her to be taken to the hospital at Mongar some time before the delivery was due, and maybe the doctors could have saved her life. To me it seems so unnecessary, and I cannot think what else I could have done. I write the following afterwards to get it out of my system.

Their home was just a bamboo shack upon a hill,
With barely the necessities of life within.
A few wooden boxes, a couple of shelves,
A fireplace, pots and pans, and a ladle or two.
The floor space was hardly big enough
For the four of them to lie side-by-side,
But they needed to keep close on the cold nights,

Otherwise there was no way to keep warm.
Cobwebs hung from the roof, thick with soot,
Like black tentacles hanging down, evilly
Waiting to catch some unsuspecting soul.
But at first it wasn't this that brought out in me
Irritation, disgust, desperate anger, frustration.
The woman who lay sick on the bare floorboards,
With only a dirty cloth as covering.
Her face was pale with weariness and pain,
And eyes filled with fear and dark despair.
How was she going to care for the new baby,
With all its needs and helplessness?
Her hands were clawed, some fingers gone.
Her feet twisted and shortened, she was hardly able to walk.
Her face on one side was paralysed and that eye was unable to close.
Her crippled hands, with no sensation,
How would they cater to a baby's needs?
How rough she would be, without knowing,
Often hurting the innocent one, without realising.
Why God? Why do they act so irresponsibly?
Bringing a new baby into this situation?
Love may be there, but no tenderness, no gentleness.
Why bring a baby into the hardness and squalor of this?
Is there no justice in life at all?
These thoughts all crossed my mind,
With confusion and anger, that God allowed it.
Then His voice came through the confusion.
'She is a child of My creation.
Because of her disease has she no right
To love and be loved, to live as normal a life
As you or any other human being?
Has she not suffered enough with her disease?
With the poverty and squalor of her life?

With the knowledge that people don't want her?
That she is an embarrassment upon society?
Why should she not love and be loved?
Why should she not have joy as she looks upon her baby
Lying whole and healthy in her arms?
She and others like her, why should they not
Live life to the full, and enjoy all I give?'
Then my eyes were opened, and my heart responded to the voice of God.
Why indeed should they abstain from living normal lives?
God forgive me for those unkind, uncaring thoughts.
And then I thought, yes how wonderful it will be
To see her face light up with joy when the baby is born
And lying contentedly in her arms, all pain forgotten.
My heart rejoiced then for the joy that was to be hers.
But it did not happen, the baby was not born, the mother died
Still with the look of fear and despair within her eyes.
Why, Lord? Why? And what about the orphans left behind?
The only comfort is that God is Sovereign.
He does what is best for us, and does it in love.
He says, 'You don't understand now, but later you will.'
With that, the questions are silenced,
And as time goes on, the hurts heal.

Upon enquiring, I find that she has a brother who is married, and the two children will be able to live with him and his family. We suggest they be enrolled in the local school, and we help with their uniform and other expenses for as long as we work in the area. It is always difficult to understand why, when we pray, some people are healed and others are not.

There has been quite a lot of wildlife around us, apart from the fleas, flies and leeches! We have a leopard prowling around for a while and one night he demolishes a goat belonging to one of the staff. We all wish we had eaten the goat first! Then a bear with her cub takes residence on a small hill opposite us. They are there for some weeks and eventually move on. Barking deer are here all through the year, and come into the garden, sometimes ruining our vegetables, as do the wild boar, but they make a bigger mess of things. There is also a wild goat that roams around here and seems to live on the hill above us. I think I enjoy watching the otters in the river most of all. We see them whenever we are down near the river and they seem to really enjoy life! We also have lodgers in our roof, in the form of a pair of falcons and their four chicks, which at the moment are just little balls of fluff, but always hungry and starting to grow. It is tough on our dog who is often dive-bombed by the mother falcon. One chick injures a wing learning to fly. Joyce rescues it more than once, putting it back on the ledge to be fed. It does eventually learn to fly, and we are able to identify it by its crooked wing when it soars overhead. It does not seem to hamper it. Most mornings I wake up to the most lovely birdsong, loud, rich and mellow. It is a grey-winged blackbird that is perched on a branch not far from my window.

Over the time we have been here, we have been looking for a suitable place for the very disabled leprosy patients, where they can have more care. Between here and Mongar there is a Basic Health Unit that has enough flat land around it to build some suitable accommodation for them, so we arrange for this to be done. Some of the patients have families and their own bit of land, so at first it is only six disabled ones who live on their own who move. We supply them with rice and other things every month, and the health worker gives them their medicines, which we issue to him regularly. It takes about 8-9 hours' walk to get there, but it is just by the mule track that we follow to Mongar.

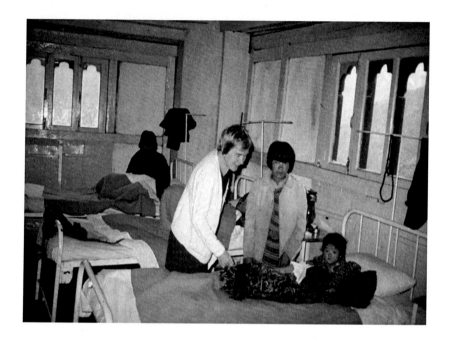

The Government has recently started a National Leprosy Eradication Campaign: the aim is to control leprosy and finally eradicate it from the whole country, a very ambitious scheme but one dear to our hearts. We have heard about the new treatment which is a multi-drug therapy (MDT) consisting of Rifampicin, to be given under supervision once a month; Lamprene – a large dose monthly also under supervision and a smaller dose daily – together with our usual leprosy drug, Dapsone. We are asked to do a pilot scheme here and have to start with twenty patients at a time, who stay at the hospital for the first month. At the start of the programme, the youngest sister of His Majesty the King comes with her cousin to spend a few days. The first day she speaks to the patients and some of the village headmen and then comes and has tea with us. The next day she and her cousin stay all morning with us, helping out where needed, including doing dressings on some of the patients. They seem very interested in what is going on, asking lots of questions. Two of the patients that we start on MDT are young lads of about 13 and 16, who were recently detected and highly positive. We are always glad to find these young folk early, to help prevent the disabilities that occur so often in untreated patients.

All the repairs and alterations are eventually finished at the hospital, and best of all, the clean water supply is up and running. It is wonderful. We now wash dirt out of our clothes instead of adding to it!

There is a wild addition to our household at present. She is a lovely red panda that an old man has found in a nearby forest and brought to us. We have her for a few days as she seems very thin and weak, and find she loves sweet biscuits! She soon goes off back to the wild, which is good.

The village work, although very hard-going and strenuous, is very satisfying, and there is so much to enjoy as we walk in this amazing country. The orchids grow in profusion in some areas and, depending on the altitude, there are many different kinds of flowers and bushes. Sometimes it is like walking through a very large rockery where different kinds of ferns grow, some small and lacy and others large. There are many small flowers that appear to grow straight out of the rocks. This country is probably a botanist's delight. We also see quite a bit of wildlife. The otters in the rivers I have mentioned before, but one day we watch a large group of them as they play and fish on the opposite side of the river; there are at least 25 of them and they seem to be really enjoying life. We also see Himalayan martens quite often, along with different kinds of monkeys and deer. One day, a group of wild boar goes charging down the hill about a hundred yards in front of us, which is not so pleasant. We have had patients in the different hospitals who have suffered nasty injuries from these boars.

Gentians and Orchid

I am walking back with a few of the lads once after doing some village work when we come to a landslide, which is not unusual, but this one still seems to be slipping. Anyway, we decide we should be able to get across, not that there is any other option, so we set off and suddenly I feel myself sliding down at quite a pace. As I start, one of the paramedical workers grabs my hand and slips with me, and we cannot stop. I see the funny side of it, and start to laugh until the paramedical reminds me that a few hundred feet below us is a very large river. Fortunately, we eventually come to a stop by a fallen tree that is lodged in the earth, so we start to climb up, but it is quite tortuous as we take a few steps upwards and then slip back a few. All this time we are hearing shouts of encouragement from the others, who form a chain as we get nearer to help us up the last little bit!

It feels safer to me to travel by foot rather than vehicle sometimes: the roads are narrow and there are often landslides and sharp bends, and looking down, there is usually a steep drop to a roaring river! As the new road is progressing, we are able to leave the jeep fairly near the end of the completed section, so that we can reach Mongar more quickly. One day I set off to Mongar with a driver and two paramedical workers who are going to do some village work. We follow the mule track until we reach the road and then carry on in the jeep. We drop the paramedical workers off and travel on a bit further until we come to a large rock in the road. The driver thinks he can just get round it, and he puts his head out to make sure we are not too close to the edge, and I put my head out of the passenger window to make sure we do not bash into the rock. There is a smell of burning, and as I look, I see a wire coming out of the rock! I put my head in quickly and tell the driver the road workers are blasting. I have not finished telling him when there is an almighty explosion and the jeep rocks about as rocks and dust fall all around us. The amazing thing is that only the back windows of the jeep are broken and neither of us is hurt, only rather shaken. Our two colleagues come running up, having heard the explosion and expect us both to be injured. They are as happy as we are to be safe. We are so thankful to God for His protection, and to all the people who often pray for travelling mercies for us! Usually, when any blasting is taking place, there is a man waving a red flag some distance from where it is happening, so our experience is not a normal occurrence.

About this time we have to go to Thimphu for some business, and also to meet a new doctor and his wife who are coming to work in Mongar. A few hours after we set off on the journey, snow starts to fall and it continues most of the way. We have to stop and clear bits of the road occasionally to get through, and consequently do not get as far as we have planned for the first night, so we stay in a bamboo hut. We are so cold in spite of wearing all our clothes and curling up in our sleeping bags, and it feels perishing! The altitude is about 9,500 feet, and someone tries to light a fire in an old tin box which does not produce very much except smoke! We survive and the following nights are not so bad. The snow looks beautiful, covering the trees and hills as we travel along. The lateral road through Bhutan goes over a number of high passes, the highest one being about 12,400 feet.

We do all we have to do in Thimphu, meet up with the new workers, John and Hilary Burslem, and introduce them to the Director of Health Services and others, and then set off on the return journey. Apart from trouble getting the vehicle to start every morning, we manage reasonably well. In cold weather the diesel solidifies and so, to soften it, the driver lights a fire underneath for a while. It sounds horrific, but most drivers in these mountains use the same method. When we come towards the highest pass, Thrumsingla, the snow becomes deeper and deeper. We take out the spades and shovels and set about trying to clear a way through with the help of three road labourers. They tell us the pass is only 2 km away, and as it is just mid-morning, we all set to work, taking it in turns with the spades, pushing the vehicle and inching towards the pass. By midday we are all drooping considerably, apart from John, and still the pass cannot be seen. Joyce goes on a bit to light a fire and try to make some tea, but it takes her 1½ hours, because the wood is wet and the snow takes ages to melt. We have a very welcome drink eventually and set to work again. The snow is up to our knees, it is difficult to walk and everything is an effort as the air is so thin. We finally reach the pass at 4 pm; it has taken six hours to go 2 km! The other side of the pass is on the south side and the snow is much less thick so we are able to carry on more easily. About three hours or so later, we arrive at a road maintenance camp where we are able to spend the night. We sit around a wood-burning stove to warm up and dry out: it is bliss! We arrive back without any problems the next day.

Joyce has been asked if she will to return to Mongar for a time as they are very busy, and do not have a senior nurse. Another nurse from England is due to arrive shortly and the plan is for her to join me in Lhuntse. Joyce accompanies her up from Mongar, but soon after she arrives, a forest fire sends the three of us out in a hurry. The flames are racing up the hill towards our house and we try to quench or divert them. We release the horses which are terrified, and are joined by the rest of the staff and some local people. Eventually the flames are all extinguished and we gratefully return to our beds. We never know how the fire has started, but we know what devastation they can cause. I miss Joyce, but Rosie is good company and also a much better cook than either of us, and our diet has improved a bit! By this time, the motor road is complete and it is easier for us to get supplies up.

The Government is keen for us to set up another centre in central Bhutan, and I am asked if I will go. I am very happy where I am and have not thought of moving again, but it seems to be the right thing. The Director General of Health Services arranges to meet up with me and shows me a number of different sites we could have. We eventually decide on a place on the top of a hill where we will be nearer a good water supply and more of the local villages. The problem is that there is no connecting road, and the site is nearly 1,000 feet up from the nearest road. He says he will arrange for the road to be built if we will get on with the centre. We are able to rent a house in the village where we can live and work. In the meantime, we have to finish off in Lhuntse and hand over the work to a doctor and his wife.

Chapter Four – Yebilaptsa

Rosemary, a paramedical worker, a driver and I, with a couple of lads as general helpers, move to the centre of the country to start up the new hospital. I am sorry to move again as I have enjoyed the work and the people in Lhuntse, but there seems to be no one else to start this work. We rent a house in the village called Tingtingbhi, with two rooms for the dispensary and two other rooms for two married staff and their families to live. Upstairs, Rosemary has a room in the front and I have an adjoining room at the back, where we also keep our belongings. Rosie's room doubles as the 'best' room, where visitors are entertained! The other two rooms are shared by the two lads and any other staff who arrive before the hospital is built. We all hope it will not be too long!

The village is at an altitude of just over 2,000 feet and seems very hot to us all. We are told the name means literally 'a flat place in a hole' – and this seems to sum it up perfectly. It is surrounded by hills and feels quite airless after the breezy places we have lived in. We begin to refer to it as The Hole! The best thing for us is the river which is not too far away, so most days we all go to cool off in the river, and since there is no water or bathroom in the house until later in our stay, we wash our clothes and ourselves in the river, and always take two large plastic drums with us to fill and take back to the house to use for cooking, etc. We are so grateful for the river's proximity. We also find out that our driver loves fishing, and when he catches anything, we all benefit! The wives of the two staff suggest they cook for us all, for which we are very grateful. I think it must be the pumpkin season, for apart from the occasional fish we have rice, pumpkin and chillies and lentils every day for many, many weeks! It is not the easiest situation for anyone, especially the married couples – and Rosie, who has not lived in such a situation before, but apart from the heat, she takes it all pretty calmly.

After we have been there for a few months, I mention to Rosie how wonderful it would be if we could have some cake. There is nothing sweet in our diet, and I always had a sweet tooth! We just laugh at the thought and get on with the day. That evening, the head man of the village, who owns the house we are renting, comes over with a box in his hand and says he has been down to Calcutta in India for some days, and has brought me back a cake! We can hardly believe our eyes! It probably took him three or four days to get back, but the cake tastes like nectar to us!

Patients start coming straightaway and we deal with them as best we can. The hospital is being built on one of the hills about 1,000 feet or so higher than the village. I have arranged a building contractor and he organises the builders and labourers, who all live in little shacks at the building site. It is a lovely site, amongst the pine trees and with a beautiful view down the river. Until the road is built all the supplies have to be carried up. I go up once or twice a week to check it out, sort out any problems if I can, and treat any of the workers who are sick. Because of the lower altitude, there is more malaria and other tropical diseases here.

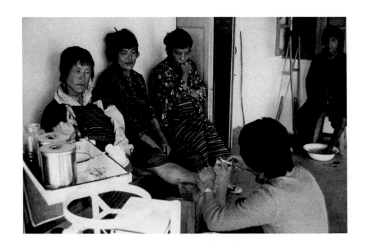

We look after five districts for leprosy control, all of which contain a number of languages. Two of these districts are in mainly Nepali-speaking areas while the other three areas use Bhutanese languages. We are in Kheng District and I believe it is one of the poorest in Bhutan; again, it has a completely different language from the other three places. There are two paramedical workers, who have been based in different districts for some time, but we are sending three more for training, and we will also need staff for the hospital.

With the lower altitude, some of the birds and other wildlife around here are different. There are tiny sunbirds, great hornbills and many others in between. This is also about the only area where golden langurs are seen – and there are many around here. We also see flying squirrels and occasionally a porcupine, and then there are barking deer, leopards and, of course, otters in the river.

I do a short village trip south from here at the end of the rainy season. I find it very hot, wet and tiring. We go through forests and streams, and leeches really feast off our blood, but it is very interesting to see the differences in this area, and also the people's way of life. They live mainly in bamboo houses, some raised off the ground, and they certainly seem to be poorer than those elsewhere in Bhutan, and have lots of diseases. Whenever we stop, patients come with different conditions for treatment. When asked what is wrong, some people say they want medicines for diarrhoea or a cough or whatever it is, and when asked how long they have had it, answer, 'I haven't got it now, but I need the medicine for when I get it, as you will not be here then!'

Rosie falls ill with hepatitis which is a long drawn-out affair and this is not the best place to fall sick. Since the building work is going on apace, and some of the houses and some of the hospital buildings are nearly ready, we decide she should move up to Yebilaptsa, the hospital site, where it is cooler and more pleasant for her. This means I also have to move up to get meals for her, etc., and then I have to go down in the mornings, which is lovely in the cool air with the birds singing, but going up and down like this becomes more of a struggle as the day wears on. I often try to go up to get her lunch at midday, and come back down again until the day's work is done. Walking up the steep thousand feet again in the evening is sometimes hard going! Now, with more of the accommodation complete, we decide to use one house as the dispensary and deal with patients there. The rest of the staff also move up, and all the equipment and medicines are carried up, but we have to leave the jeep down in the village until the road is complete.

We have not been there very long when, as I am examining a patient, suddenly all the medicine bottles and jars and things on the shelves start to jump up and down and it is hard to stand. We all rush out and wait until the quake has finished and then pick up the things that have fallen and get on with what we are doing. It is not the only quake we have, but fortunately none of the buildings are ever damaged.

As soon as the hospital buildings are complete, we fit them out with beds and the equipment we have, and soon every bed is filled. As with the other places, there is a wide variety of diseases here, so there are patients with leprosy and TB, dysenteries, malaria, skin diseases, along with children and adults with heart diseases and chest infections, and sometimes a child with meningitis. We also get patients we have not been able to diagnose, who fortunately seem to get better! There are usually patients with injuries of different kinds. We send two girls and two boys who have just finished at school for nurse technicians' training in India, and we look forward to their return. When the road is complete, we are able to bring up the rest of the equipment and stuff we need.

From the time we began our work in this country, we always held morning prayers before we started work, to ask for wisdom and help in all we had to do. This seemed more important when we worked in isolated areas. Throughout the years others joined us, and sometimes some of the patients also came.

It is almost time for Christmas, and although it is not a public holiday here, we always try to celebrate. This year we decide to have a party for all the labourers working on the hospital, and their families. One of the lads manages to buy a pig, and between them it is slaughtered and cooked, together with plenty of rice, chillies and vegetables. They all come with their plates, as do the staff and their families, and all the patients. We sit around in a large circle on the ground and the food is dished out to everyone. It is a happy time for all of us, and everyone especially appreciates having meat to eat!

Work on the water supply

Joyce joins us as soon as there are sufficient senior nurses in Mongar, and it is great to be working with her again. The road is complete but the water supply is not. At the moment, we have a pipe fixed into the stream which runs down to the hospital. It works fairly well except when the rats chew it, or the monkeys move it! So one of the first things Joyce does is to organise a more secure supply until the water tank and all the pipe-work is complete, which makes life easier. She is a whiz at DIY and we call on her regularly when anything needs fixing!

The time comes for me to go to visit some of the areas where there are quite a number of patients. The weather is fine when we leave but, when we have been walking for an hour or two, it starts to rain. It pours so heavily that it comes straight through my umbrella, which I thought was a good one! We stop to eat our lunch in a village house, and the lady of the house kindly makes us some Bhutanese tea, which consists of tea, butter and salt churned up well with hot water. This gives us added strength for the rest of the journey. We continue in the rain, slipping and sliding through the mud, again with leeches feasting on our blood! The rain stops just before we reach our destination for the night, but we are all soaked to the skin. The house we stay in has only one room, so it is not possible to change, apart from our socks! We see all the patients who turn up, and more come along during the evening. Eventually we have our meal of rice, etc. and then spread out on the floor to sleep. It is a bit noisy as the pigs are grunting and snuffling underneath the bamboo floor, the chickens are scratching in the roof, and the rats scrabbling in our belongings! We see more patients in the morning and then set off again in the rain, until we reach our next destination, which is a dispensary where one of our paramedical workers stays. Here we change out of our wet things before we see any patients. There are a lot of leprosy patients in this area, and we manage to see and examine most of them.

We take on a number of young men, all in their teens, who have just finished school and who want some kind of training. While they help around the hospital, we can see what kind of work will be suitable for them. They are all willing and helpful, and all speak a reasonable amount of English. One of these lads always amuses me with his use of English. One day he comes to me and says, 'Sister, I have done a very great mischief; I am very sorry.' On enquiring what this great mischief is, it turns out he has broken a glass thermometer! He does not realise how many glass thermometers I have broken in my life! Another time he comes and says, 'Sister, the Vim powder is exhausted.' It takes me a minute or two to work out that the tin is empty! He eventually goes to the Health School in Thimphu, is given dentistry training, and then sent to another part of Bhutan.

We keep a few chickens that we have acquired, and one of the hens becomes broody and starts to sit on her eggs. They are just about ready to hatch when we hear a terrible noise coming from the run. We go to see what is going on and find a cobra in the run, slowly swallowing all the eggs, and the poor chickens are terrified. A couple of staff also come to see what is happening, one of them carrying a stick. He hits the snake, and immediately it starts coughing up the eggs and then disappears. One of the eggs cracks and out pops a baby chick! A real Jonah story, but the chick grows and starts laying eggs eventually.

The water supply is finally completed, we have no trouble with it, and we are all very happy to have water running from our taps. Then one day we find very little water coming out, so we send up a couple of men to check the tank. We have just finished our lunch when they return. We smell them before we see them! They carry a long pole to which they have tied the decomposing body of a deer, hence the putrid smell. The water tank has a bamboo roof, and the deer must have jumped onto it and gone straight through into the tank and drowned. How long it has been in the tank is anyone's guess! We have all been happily drinking the water, bathing in it and cooking with it without any ill effects, but when we see and smell the poor thing, it certainly turns our stomachs! After this, and after the tank is cleaned out, we arrange a solid roof for it.

The staff seem to be interested in many different things and frequently ask questions. We asked them if they would like to come to our house one evening with all their questions which, between us, we would attempt to answer. We arranged the evening and quite a number of them came. Their questions covered all manner of things – medical, our faith, the mission, etc., and the evenings were repeated every now and then.

Joyce starts a sewing class for the ladies who really enjoy learning to make clothes for their children, and before long the small girls are showing off their new dresses!

Many of the staff we have live away from home, apart from some of the Bhutanese staff, and they are all fairly young, so we arrange an area to make a badminton court and volleyball court, and also manage to get hold of a table tennis table and build a bamboo shack for it. The Bhutanese play a lot of archery, so in the evenings there are different things for them to do, and the wives and children go to cheer them on. We also enjoy watching them. Joyce plays badminton and we all enjoy a game of table tennis from time to time. We also have picnics by the river sometimes, which are enjoyed by everyone. Fairly often, one of the staff, usually one of the young men, will come and ask us to go to their house and pray for a relative or friend, or sometimes it is for a patient in the ward. We are happy to do this, and if it is for a very sick patient, a number of the staff also join us. We sometimes see quick answers, but not always.

Following the earlier trials in Lhuntsi, the Government decides to follow the WHO recommendations and implement multi-drug therapy (MDT) nationally, so we are asked to start this in our areas. Until recently, patients were given one drug, Dapsone, that they had to take daily, usually for the rest of their lives, and there was no real hope of a cure. Now they are to have the three drugs of multi-drug therapy, and the multibacillary patients will take them for two years, and the paucibacillary patients for just six months. Because the two new drugs Rifampicin and Lamprene are given as supervised doses, one health worker has to see each patient every month, which entails a lot of extra work, especially for the paramedical workers. I was unsure whether they would want to take on more, as they already did a tremendous amount of trekking around the villages, seeing patients every three months. So I held a meeting with them where we discussed all the issues, and gave them the option of covering half of the areas first and when they were complete, doing the rest. They were very enthusiastic and all of them wanted every patient to have the opportunity to take the MDT treatment at the same time. I was very thrilled and proud of them. These fellows walked so much that they had to buy two or three new pairs of shoes every year, so it was not an easy option for them. Now there is a definite end in view, patients have the hope of a cure, and all of us who have worked for any time with leprosy patients are excited. Is it possible that we will see a world without leprosy?

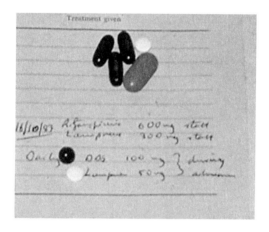

MDT pills

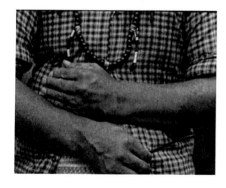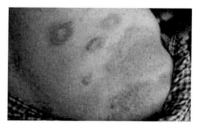

Healing lesions on a multibacillary leprosy patient

Every now and then we have to travel to Thimphu for meetings, shopping or other business. We have a very good driver who is also a mechanic, so if the vehicle breaks down he can usually fix it. He is also a good fisherman, and on the road from east to west we cross many rivers, so he likes to stop at one of these. While Joyce and I light a fire and cook rice, he wades into the river, usually in his shoes and socks, carrying an old tin with nylon thread around it and a hook on the end, and proceeds to catch a few fish. This river has rainbow trout and he soon has enough for our meal. He cleans and fries them and before long we are enjoying a great meal. We are always amused as, when he catches the fish, he puts them down into the socks he is wearing, and then when he has caught enough, wades out of the river, pulls the fish out of his socks, begins to clean them, and then fries them. He continues the journey wearing his wet socks and shoes!

As time goes by, we are very encouraged by the different changes we have seen in people, even in only a few months in some cases. Physically some patients are brought to the hospital as a last resort; they have tried everything else and nothing has helped them. One woman comes with tuberculosis which she must have had for some time, and she only weighs 35 kg. She is skin and bone. We put her onto TB medicine and a decent diet and in two months she gains another 12 kg and looks and feels a different person. One new leprosy patient is very sick and unhappy when he is admitted, and never smiles, but in about 3-4 weeks he turns out to be a friendly, grateful old man, who is so pleased to be free from pain. He then spends his time, before returning home, going round trying to cheer up other patients. It is so encouraging to see the changes in people, and we marvel at the way God has been at work making people whole. We pray for patients, especially when we are not sure of the diagnosis, and when they are very sick and we are always thrilled when they recover.

One day we leave to go to the northern part of the district which we have not surveyed fully. It is a long trek and we stay in a different village each night on the way. In each one, there are always many patients needing treatment as well as those with leprosy. In one of these villages, a young man comes in with a tourniquet on his arm, his hand very swollen and discoloured. He has been bitten by a snake, and once the tourniquet is on, no one will take it off until the limb shrivels up. I have seen a number of young people who lost their legs in this way. There are poisonous snakes in Bhutan, but many of them are not, but even so I have to spend a lot of time persuading the people to let me take this tourniquet off. Reluctantly they let me, and I clean the arm up, and get him to try to move his fingers. He is in a lot of pain, so I give him some pain killers, and ask him to come back in the morning. In the meantime I hope and pray that I have done the right thing. I am pretty sure he will be all right as I find out that the tourniquet was not put on immediately after the bite. So in the morning he returns: some of the swelling has gone down, and he looks relieved and happy. The hand is still discoloured, and I tell him to exercise his fingers often, and before long he recovers, regaining full use of his hand.

In the next village where we stop for the night, we are inundated with patients, and it takes us hours to see them all, but finally they go and we clear up. Then one of the paramedical workers comes to me and says, 'We have been given 70 eggs, and tonight you must have a momelette!' 'Thank you,' I answer, 'but only two eggs in it, and we can boil a few to eat on the way tomorrow.' A bit later he returns with an enormous 'momelette', and says that they used only twelve eggs to make it! I cut it in half and he takes the rest.

Rosie comes back from a trip with a hair-raising story. She has been driving down a hill, round hairpin bends, when suddenly the steering wheel comes off in her hands! A big pile of rocks right on the edge of the road stops the jeep from going over the edge down a few hundred feet to the river below. How we thank God for her protection.

There is one area south of us that we have not been able to cover very well, so I go with two teams of paramedical workers to try to cover the whole region. As well as those with leprosy and TB, we find many other sick people to deal with, and it takes us about fifteen days to complete the area, staying each night at a different place as we go. On the last day, as we are completing the work, one of the paramedical workers tells me that there is a guest house on the other side of the river, and we could probably stay there for the night.

We are near the border with India, and the whole area is a game reserve. Someone comes over from the other side of the river in an old dugout canoe and takes us across, and we go to see the Ranger. He says we can spend the night in the guest house – and also offers us an elephant to take us through the reserve to the nearest motor road in Bhutan! I am not able to go via India without applying for a special permit, and we have to get those from Thimphu. So it sounds marvellous to me: first, a night in a bed, and then being able to get home the next day, instead of five more days of walking! We have to be ready by 5 am, when the elephant and the mahout will be waiting for us, but he will not be able to take all of us, so some of the others will have the long trek back with the ponies.

Before dawn next day, we set off and it really is quite magical travelling through the forest as it becomes light, hearing the myriad bird songs and the calls of different animals. The morning mist rises up through the trees, as the sun starts to shine, and we have all the fresh morning scents. From the top of the elephant it is so easy to view many different kinds of deer and monkeys, wild boar, porcupine and leopards. We also see the footprints of a tiger, but never actually see one. We continue for five hours until we arrive at a logging camp, where we have to change elephants, and we cook the usual meal of rice and chillies. It is good to stretch our legs for a bit, as we just sit astride the elephant on some old sacking. We set off again, but now we have to take a guard with a gun as they say it is a dangerous area! We continue to see plenty of wildlife, including a large herd of wild elephants, and eventually, another five hours later, reach our destination. It is such an amazing trip, never to be forgotten. We then have a 3-4 hour road trip back to the hospital at Yebilaptsa.

We are slowly taking leprosy patients off treatment as they finish their course of multi-drug therapy, although we continue to check them once a year for a few years. The overall number of patients taking treatment is reducing year by year, although we still find a few new patients. It is a great time! Patients are happy as they now have some hope of a cure and an end to the treatment, and the paramedical workers' workload is slightly reduced. We begin to think about the retraining of some of the paramedical workers in different disciplines. Some have their own ideas of what they would like to do, and we also look at the future needs of the hospital.

A few of the leprosy patients live in little houses that often leak, and when there is a storm, part of the building collapses. When they are disabled, it is very difficult for them to repair the house or rebuild it. Over the years, we have arranged for some to be rebuilt or repaired, which has improved the lives of the patients considerably. One very disabled old man is so happy to move out of his broken-down home and move into the new one, that he tells Joyce it is like being in heaven!

Over the years in Bhutan, I often travel along the 'lateral road' which is constructed from west to east, and was completed when I worked in Mongar. It is an amazing feat of engineering that goes up to a number of high passes and down into the valleys, always with many spectacular views. Many times I travel with Joyce and we soon learn to have enough food and pots for cooking, spades and shovels, bedding and at least one spare tyre and a jerry can of diesel! We are often held up by landslides, especially when the road first opens, and on a number of occasions we are stuck in between two landslides, so until one is cleared it is impossible to move on. We sometimes have to sleep in the vehicle or a bamboo shack, and once in the snow on one of the higher passes we have to put a tent up: it is freezing cold! Along the way there are many flowering bushes and trees, and we often stop to look at flowers growing near the road, especially the orchids. Over quite a long section there are masses of rhododendron in the spring, both bushes and trees of all different colours, a real picture. There are also magnificent magnolias growing on very tall trees. I once pick up some petals from the ground and they are the size of my hand. One autumn, as we travel over the lateral road, everything in one area is a mass of reds, oranges, yellows and browns, and each time we round a bend we are treated with a fresh riot of colours. It is glorious! Joyce, who loves flowers and plants more than I do, will suddenly shout, 'Stop, stop!' as she wants to see everything more closely and take photos, so the journey sometimes takes a bit longer than usual.

We have a great team of staff here: Bhutanese, some Nepalis, and one Indian family. They all seem to get on extremely well, and we rarely have any disputes, which is amazing. The majority are hard workers, and have a very good attitude to the patients. Most of them we have known since they left school, and were able to arrange their training for them, and it is so good to see how they have matured and become responsible members of the community. Now most of them are married and have families, and of course we delivered the children as they arrived! It is lovely to see them all progressing so well.

Some of the team

Postscript

Time rolled by and I was in my eighteenth year in the country, having worked in four different areas. I was very settled with good friends, great colleagues and a very satisfying job, and could not imagine doing anything else for the following years up to my retirement, although I found the village work, where there was no motor road, very strenuous. So it came as a bombshell to be asked if I would be willing to take on the post of Director of Personnel based in The Leprosy Mission's International Office in London.

All the staff had received a letter from the office asking if there was anyone within the mission we would like to nominate for the post, but I never imagined myself in the job. My immediate reaction was no, it is not for me, and I put it out of my mind. Then, when visiting a Swiss friend and telling him my thoughts on it (that I was not suitable, did not consider myself able or good enough for it, did not know anything about it, and so how could I possibly do a big job like that?), he was not impressed! He pointed out that, when my name had been nominated by people who knew me, and considered me the right person for the job, the least I should do was to look into it, talk it over with the boss, and think seriously and pray about it! So after discussion, thought and prayer, I came to the decision that this should be the next step for me. Over the years, I have experienced the utter faithfulness of God in everything, especially in His protection, His provision and His patient teaching. But I viewed the future with great trepidation. Although we had had regular home leaves, it was more than 26 years since I had actually worked in England.

By now, leprosy was more or less under control in Bhutan. Many people's lives had been changed physically, mentally and spiritually. Over the years there had been great developments in roads, health, education, agriculture and other infrastructure. I consider it a great privilege as well as a unique opportunity to have worked in Bhutan in the early days of its development, and to have had a small hand in it. So when I left, I felt as if the leaving was the biggest sacrifice I had ever made in my life. Eventually, eighteen wonderful years of hard but satisfying work in an amazing country came to an end.

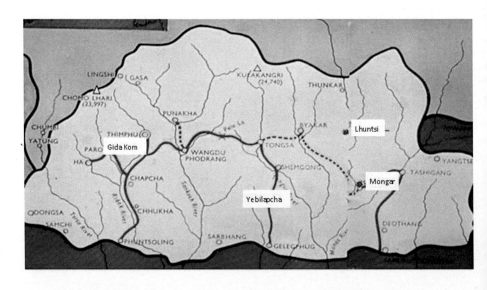

Map of Bhutan showing The Leprosy Mission Hospital sites